CREATED BY SCOTT CLARKE

copyright 2017

GO
NAVY!!!!!

OUTPERFORM, OUTSMART, OUTSHINE AND OUTLAST...

AND WHEN ALL'S SAID AND DONE YOU CAN KISS OUR GRASS!

MAKE-UP TIPS

AIN'T JUST FOR THE LADIES, HERE'S A TIP FOR SOME "MAKE-UP GO NAVY"

SEAFOOD, SEA
AND SAILOR'S BABY...
BUT FOOTBALL'S
WHY I SAY GO NAVY!

NAVY
FOOTBALL
IS...
CRABSOLUTELY
CRABULOUS!

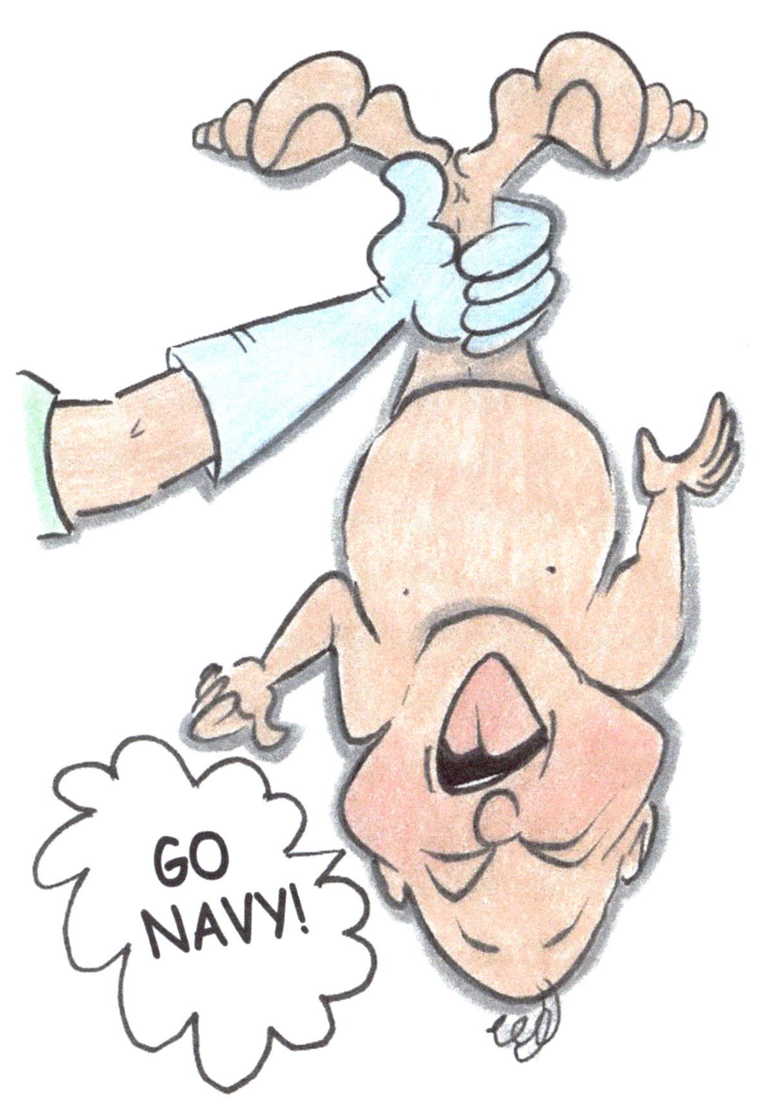

BORN TO WIN AND KEEP ON WINNING,
WE'RE NAVY FANS FROM THE BEGINNING!

EAT, DRINK
AND
GO NAVY!

IT AIN'T ATTITUDE!

IT'S ANNAPTITUDE!

ANNAPOLIS MARYLAND

N
NAVY GALS
DO IT BETTER!

GO NAVY
MARYLAND IS FOR CRABS!!
ANNAPOLIS MARYLAND
NAVY

GO NAVY
?
BEAT ARMY

I'M REALLY NOT CRAZY, AND I'M NOT INSANE.. BUT I SEE "GO NAVY" IN MY VARICOSE VEINS!
N

ARMY
CRUSH THE
COMPETITION

OLD NAVY AIN'T TEE SHIRTS, JACKETS OR JEANS, OLD NAVY IS "GO NAVY" FANS LIKE ME!
N

GOT ANY ACES?
GO NAVY

GO NAVY!
NAVY
N
GOT TEAM SPIRIT?

GO NAVY PLAY THAT GAME, TO WATCH YOU WIN IS WHY WE CAME!

GO NAVY
I CAUGHT CRABS IN ANNAPOLIS MARYLAND
GOT CRABS?
MARYLAND IS FOR CRABS
ANNAPOLIS MARYLAND

N
GO
NAVY
...BEAT ARMY

SHARE
YOUR
PASSION
FOR
GO
NAVY
FASHION
N
N
N

DISGO NAVY!

SOME LIKE BINGO AND A
CHEAP BUFFET...
BUT NAVY FOOTBALL
IS WHAT MAKES OUR DAY

ANNAPOLIS
MARYLAND

N

I'M NOT INTO DIAMONDS OR DAISIES, NAVY FOOTBALL IS WHAT DRIVES ME CRAZY!
N

ANNAPOLIS
MARYLAND,
HOME OF
THE GAME,
WHERE NAVY
PLAYS ARMY
AND PUTS
THEM TO
SHAME!

I LOVE TO VISIT THE ANNAPOLIS DOCKS BUT NAVY FOOTBALL IS WHAT REALLY ROCKS!

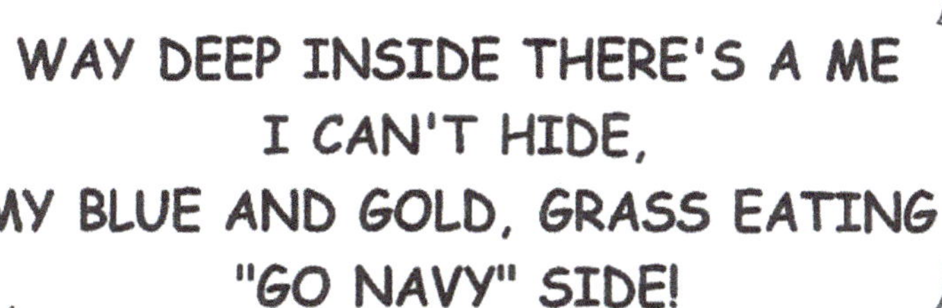

WAY DEEP INSIDE THERE'S A ME
I CAN'T HIDE,
MY BLUE AND GOLD, GRASS EATING
"GO NAVY" SIDE!

N

LOVE GETS
OLD AND
MONEY
RUNS OUT,
BUT NAVY
FOOTBALL
STILL MAKES
ME SHOUT!

N

SHOW YOUR TEAM SPIRIT,
SHOW YOUR TEAM PRIDE,
YELL, SCREAM AND SHOUT
SHOW YOUR "GO NAVY" SIDE!

NAVY

COME CLIMB ABOARD,
TAKE THE GOAT FOR A RIDE,
GIVE IT A TRY,
SHOW YOUR "GO NAVY" SIDE!

I LOVE
YOU,
I WANT
YOU,
I NEED
YOU BABY,
BUT DARLIN'
WE'RE THROUGH
UNLESS YOU
GO NAVY!!!

SHOW SOME
TEAM SPIRIT
START OFF
WITH A CHEER,
AND IF ALL
ELSE FAILS
JUST GO BUY
MORE BEER!

GO NAVY

GOT NAVY?

HAVE FAITH, BE COURAGEOUS AND DON'T GIVE UP HOPE...
N
AND NEVER EVER LET'EM GET YOUR GOAT!

About the Author....

Scott Clarke is an artist, writer and teaching artist hoping t
enlighten, inspire and entertain with his creativity.
Scott spends most of his time drawing,
writing and working as an art instructor
in addition to being a mentor through
diverse creative outreach programs.
He has a well received list of published books, assorted
collections of greeting cards and other commodities
featuring his creations. With few limits Scott
finds many outlets for his creative energy
coloring the world with love, light and laughter.
website www.scottclarkestudio.com
email scottclarkestudio@aol.com
facebook Scott Clarke
twitter @_scottclarke
instagram _scottclarke